THE ADVENTURES OF JUNGLE SWINGER.

Andrew Ure

1

ISBN 978-1-8381764-0-2

This book is dedicated to my wife Carla
and my children.

Hi ROSS, HOPE you ENJOY
THE BOOK!

27/09/2020

HOW I BECAME JUNGLE SWINGER

It was August 1977 and I was just finishing my first day of school at St James. Primary School in Coatbridge Scotland.

As I made my way to one of the exit gates of the school. I noticed that there was a group of boys waiting. As I approached them it became clear to me that they were waiting for me. I thought that being the new kid on the block that they wanted to say "hi" and get to know me a little.

Well, that's not why they were waiting for me. I had recently arrived from South Africa. after my parents had separated. My mother. my sister and I had moved back to Scotland where we were born.

The problem as it turned out was that my accent was being mistaken for another and not Scottish, and to the untrained ear it sounded more like I was foreign. That was the reason the lads were waiting for me at the end of my first day of school. They thought that I was foreign, and in the seventies in the Glasgow region that was a problem.

They did not like people who were not local and— I— in their way of thinking was foreign. Now I was about to find out what they thought of them. They approached me, and called me all kinds of things of which I will not repeat. Suffice it to say that they were very hostile and ready for a brawl.

They wanted to fight and when I asked for the reason why they informed me that it was because I was a foreign @***"*@. I tried to convince them that I was also Scottish, but they would have none of it.

There was going to be a fight, and that was that. So I squared up to them and put up my fists to begin the fight. It was then that they began to laugh at me and started to pull my hair and kick me in the face.

Now it needs to be explained that in South Africa if you fought another person you boxed them. You were never allowed to kick or pull the other persons hair.

This was frowned upon, and if you did it the crowd would have beaten you up.

So-as I waited for the crowd to intervene and sort these blokes out, it began to dawn on me that maybe they had different rules here because no one was jumping in to stop them. It turned out they did!

It was a free for all. A no holds barred fight, and I was totally unprepared for it. As I stood and protested about the way they were fighting, everyone just started laughing at me.

I ended up getting a thorough kicking that afternoon, and to top it off I was sent to the headmaster's office for six of the belt for starting a fight.

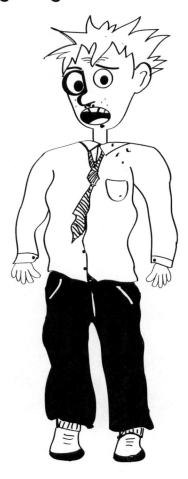

When I went home and my mother saw me, she asked what had happened, and after I told her about my welcome committee she marched straight to the school, and had it out with the headmaster. She was not too concerned about the welcome committee, as much as she was furious that I had gotten the blame, and punishment for the fight.

The headmaster was put well and truly in his place by my mom. It was an exchange of views that he would never forget!

This was my introduction to Scotland. Needless to say it was not a good beginning for me, and it tainted my image of Scotland and it's people from that moment onwards.

It made me a very angry young man and I became a violent young boy who would get them before they could get me.

Shortly after that event it became evident to me that the kids who lived in Coatbridge lived very tribal and insular lives.

They did not seem to have any appreciation or knowledge of the wider world in general.

All that they knew was what they were familiar with.

One day there was a short little bloke who was a bit of a whipper snapper and who thought that he was quite the lad.

Anyway this kid wanted to ask me questions about Africa. To them, Africa, was a place full of wild animals, and people there lived in mud huts and in trees.

They thought that we lived like Tarzan and Jane. What they did not realise was that our cities were much more modern and advanced than any of the cities in Scotland.

We lived in large houses with large gardens, and had large cars. In fact, when I moved to Scotland in the seventies it felt like they were the primitive people to me.

They would ask me if I had lions, monkeys, crocodiles and sharks. It was quite ridiculous, but because I had a bit of a wicked sense of humour, I had decided to string them along and I had some fun at their expense.

This bloke, Donny was his name was totally taken in and was convinced that we ran around in loin cloths and swung on vines from tree to tree. It was then that he coined the phrase, "you must be just like, Tarzan, one of those JUNGLE SWINGERS".

It was then that everyone laughed and started to call me "Jungle Swinger" and that became my nick name.

From that moment onwards as long as I lived in Coatbridge I was known as, Jungle Swinger!

The following are accounts of the adventures I had and what it was like to be a Jungle Swinger growing up in South Africa, in the seventies.

THE EARLY YEARS

THE JUNGLE SWINGERS

This was my crazy family in the 70's. My dad with his massive beer belly and safari suits, my annoying sister, myself and my mom who was definitely out of place living in Africa!

I suppose you could have called us the JUNGLE SWINGERS although it was me who was given the nickname.

JOHANNESBURG 1971 to 74

Chapter 1
THE MOTOR BOAT
AND HOW I LEARNT TO SWIM.

When we lived in the Johannesburg area of. South Africa, my father decided to buy himself a motor boat. I think it reminded him of his days in the Royal Navy.

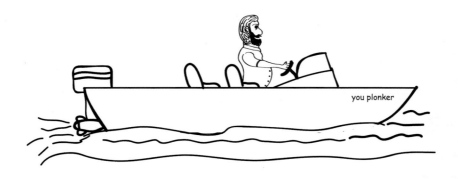

you plonker

I was four and a half when he bought the boat. We started going to the Vaal dam. The Vaal Dam is about 90km. south of Johannesburg. It was the largest body of water suitable for motor boats.

I remember that we would spend the entire day there. We would even sometimes camp over night along the shores of the dam. These were fun times, and I loved the sensation of speeding over the surface of the water. I still love that sensation to this day.

I have to say that in those days we did not have any concept of health and safety. On the contrary, we would be out on the water without life vests, and most, if not all of the adults, would be very drunk and totally oblivious of the danger that they were putting us and themselves in.

For them, this was just another opportunity to go out and have fun with plenty of booze thrown into the mix. This was normal. Despite the danger, we had some very exciting times out on the dam.

There was one time in particular, that has been etched permanently into my memories.

It was on one of these weekends, when we were out on the water that my dad had had plenty to drink, and was totally smashed out of his head, that he decided that it was time for me to learn how to swim.

He had a very unique way of teaching me how to swim. I would definitely not recommend this method to even my greatest enemy. I was four and a half years old at the time, and was about to get one of the biggest surprises of my short life.

I thought that he was going to explain to me what I would have needed to do to be able to float, and what I should do with my arms and legs when I was swimming. I also thought that he would steer the boat into the shallows so that I could learn the basics of swimming.

I was sorely mistaken! No, my dad had a completely crazy and deadly method of teaching me to swim.

Before I knew what was happening, he reached over to me, grabbed me and hurled me into the deep mirky waters of the Vaal dam.

No life vest, nothing to keep me afloat! To make maters worse–in his drunken state, my dad thought it was hilarious and sped off away from me. His way of thinking was sink or swim.

Thankfully I was able to keep myself afloat by treading water, and doing what I was later to come to know as the doggie paddle.

I will never forget that experience, and am glad to say that I never used that method to teach my children to swim.

I did however learn to swim a few months later when we lived in Robertsham Johannesburg. We lived in a gated community, in a block of flats. I really liked living there as it had a communal swimming pool.

As a young kid I used to go to the pool and watch the older kids jumping into the water, and having fun in the deep end of the pool.

I remember when we first moved into the flats that I went to the pool and had a look only to see an old bike at the bottom of the deep end of the pool. I remember I felt confused as to why a bike would be in a pool.

I was soon to find out...

They used to build ramps and have competitions to see who could jump the furthest on an old clapped out bike. That was one of the main reasons I learnt to swim.

I saw these kids taking it in turns to race down the path towards a ramp that they had made out of bricks and planks of wood.

The ramp was placed right on the edge of the pool, so that they could get as much distance to race before they hit the water during the jump. The aim was to see who could get the furthest.

This often ended in tears for some of the kids who misjudged their approach to the ramp, and lost their balance. They were only wearing swimming costumes and the ground was very unforgiving.

Many a kid went home screaming at the top of their lungs, as blood poured from their knees, elbows and face.

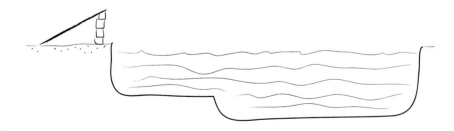

That did not put me off in the least. I was so desperate to be able to have a go, that I spent time watching how the older kids were able to swim, and then I just jumped into the deep end of the pool and copied their movements.

And yes! to my amazement and those who were watching me, I did not sink. I managed to stay afloat, and began to move slowly towards the middle of the pool.

After a few more attempts, I was able to figure out how to use my arms and legs to propel my body forward in the water. All this was so that I could have a go at the ramp at the edge of the pool.

It turned out, that I was going to be a good swimmer, and began to compete in school swimming galas. It was the only sport that I ever won a trophy for.

Chapter 2
CATS AND A SACK OF POTATOES.

When we lived in Robertsham my dad had decided that it would be good idea to get kittens for myself and my sister. According to my dad they were both little tom cats.

We loved those kittens, and they were a part of our lives. The problem with kittens is that they do not stay kittens. Our two kittens grew up quickly and before we knew it they both had turned out to be female.

This became very apparent when they both gave birth to a litter of kittens of their own within a week of each other. Before we knew it we had a flat full of cats.ten of them to be precise. Each cat had four kittens and then it became chaotic in the flat as they grew up.

As for me I loved it.

One of the drawbacks to having two female cats in the home, was that when they were on heat it attracted the tom cats from all over the neighbourhood and beyond.

The nights became a chorus of love songs from the tom cats to our two cats in the flat. We lived on the first floor and down below our balcony was a six foot high concrete wall that ran around the complex.

This became the favoured spot for the neighbourhood tom cats to perch themselves on, and start their serenading of our cats.

The noise was awful, and it always seemed to start in the early hours of the morning.

That did not go down well with my dad and the neighbours, who were being affected by that awful cats choir in the early hours.

He would be woken up in the early hours of the morning and then the french would start to flow from my grumpy and disgruntled dad.

He would open the window and throw the first thing he could get his hands on at the culprit perched on the wall below our balcony. This included old beer bottles, shoes, and ashtrays.

This proved to be a problem for my dad when it came to finding his shoes for work in the morning.

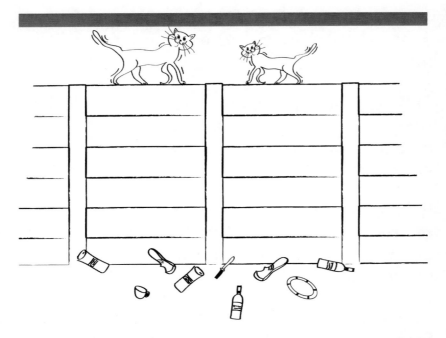

He would hunt for them until it dawned on him that maybe he had used them as missiles to get rid of the screaming tom cats.

It must have been quite amusing for the neighbours to see the evidence lying at the bottom of the fence every morning.

There would sometimes be shoes and at other

times broken bottles and, yes ,ashtrays
lying there for all to see.

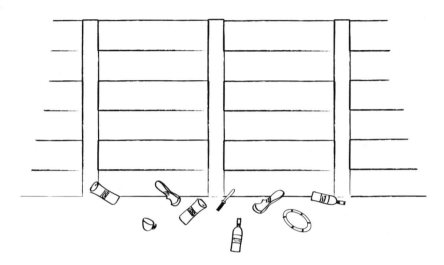

In fact that was becoming a problem as
there were only so many pairs of shoes,
bottles and ashtrays available that could
be used as missiles in his mission to get
rid of those horrendously noisy creatures.

My dad who was ever resourceful came
up with a solution. He found that a
potato was easy to grip with, and just
the right weight to throw with sufficient
force that knocked the offending cats

off the wall and kept them away for the rest of the night.

So imagine if you can, our balcony window.
There directly underneath it was a huge, 25 kilo sack of potatoes opened at the top with rather large potatoes, just waiting to be launched at the cats if they came to serenade our female cats in the early hours of the morning.

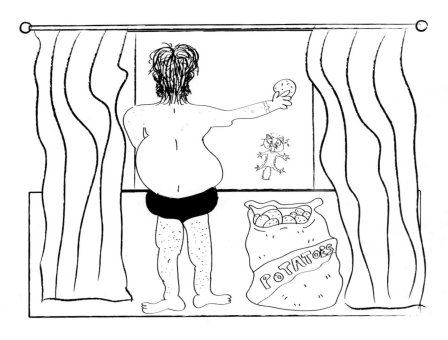

I have to say that my dad became a crack shot with those potatoes and the tom cats did not come around very often, once they had been hit with one of those spuds.

In the morning there was a fair amount of spuds lying at the base of the wall, and a good few on the other side as well. I did used to wonder what the neighbours must have thought.

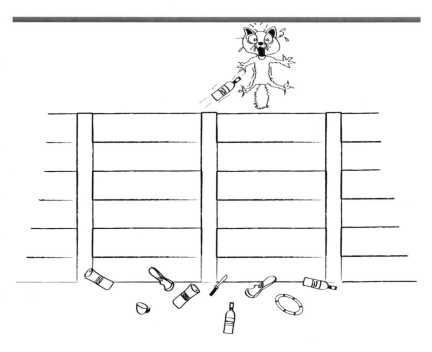

They would have thought that we were
the neighbours from hell.

Needless to say we went though a few
sacks of potatoes, but it was worth it in
the end.

Chapter 3
THE BOY WHO HATED SCHOOL

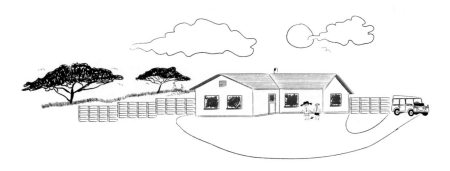

It was, 1972 and I was 5 years old. The headmaster stood in front of me and started this speech about how much he liked me, or more to the point, how much he didn't like me, but if I was a good boy then he would like me. Blaa, blaaa, blaaaa.....

I hated school.In fact, the first day of school was enough for me to make up my mind that this was a form of prison, so on the second day of school, I took my time getting my socks and shoes on. What relevance did this have?

Plenty! It was my master plan of escape. You see we lived in South Africa at the time in a town called Krugersdorp. My Father had just bought us our first and last family home.

It was a new development, so we had to travel on dirt roads to get to school. There were no buses or trains yet. A land rover used to meander over the rough terrain and came to our house to collect us. Our home was on the outskirts of the new suburb.

Every morning we would be collected at 8 am. This is where my shoes and socks came in.
Our house was the last house right on the outskirts of the development, and just over the concrete wall were the wilds of Africa! Or so it seemed to me at the time. I loved being out in the bush-veld, and for me that was my school.

The thing about the bush-veld was that the grass grew very tall, and often over a meter high

.

The grass was so tall that at my age, it was over my head, just what I needed for my plan to work.

So here is how it went down. Beauty, a rather large and jolly lady who was our home help would feed us in the morning as our parents left early to go to work. After feeding us, she would make sure we put on our school uniforms. Then we would make our way out to the front of the house and wait for the land rover to arrive.

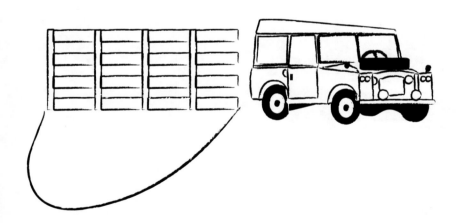

It was here, that I would put into action my master plan of escape. I decided to take my time to put my shoes and socks on. I would need to time it just right.

It all hinged on Beauty helping my sister into the land rover, as she helped her up into the vehicle I would make a break for it, and scramble over the wall, and if all went to plan "FREEDOM".

So, there I was sitting in the morning sunshine on a beautiful african day.

I waited for the sound of the land rover as it went from house to house as it collected it's little prisoners and took them away to the big horrible building. We were then herded into rooms to be educated by these strange and often nasty big people.

Why would I want to go there, when I could be out in the wild and having the time of my life playing in the bush?

Anyway, back to the plan of escape. After Beauty had helped my sister into the land rover and had made sure that she had her school bag, she turned around to help me. Who by then, had legged it over the wall and into the tall grass.

All that was left was a pair of socks and shoes, and one school suitcase. The old brown pressed cardboard ones.

I ran as fast as I could towards the trees that were by the river. Where, I planned to spend my day playing and having adventures in the sun!

In the distance I could hear Beauty shouting for me, but there was no way I was going to prison with the others. After a very long time, (about five minutes) I heard the land rover leaving our house.

It worked! My plan of escape had actually worked! But what about my shoes? There I was running, through the bush-veld with nothing to protect my feet from the harsh and rough terrain.

Well like most African children at that time, we only wore shoes to school. Otherwise we ran around barefoot all the time. So by the time I was 5 and a half , my feet were like leather and the terrain was not a problem.

So there I was all alone and in the tall grass. The thing about the bush-veld is that it was full of wild life and many of the creatures that lived in it were deadly. To name but a few.

There was no shortage of snakes and if they bit you, you had minutes to live. There were also huge spiders, scorpions and other wild creatures.

In short, a very dangerous place for a 5 and a half year old to be all by himself. Did I think that? No!!

I was more at home there than in a prison cell called a classroom. Out there I was happy as a pig in mud, of which I often was, for those two glorious weeks that, I managed to get away with this.

I was more afraid of and repulsed by the thought of going to school than by the dangers of being out there by myself for the whole day.

So, this was how my days went for those two glorious weeks. Every morning I would drag my feet and leg it over the wall.

Then I would hide in the grass and wait for the screaming and threats to stop and, then make my way to the trees that grew by the river bank.

Oh! I loved that place. The trees were just perfect for climbing and gave you a view of the whole area. I made a catapult from one of the branches and would spend hours honing my skills at target practice.

It was a wonderful place to dream and
to escape to. if there ever was danger on
the ground even at that age I could make
my way to the very top branches with
ease.

Then there was the river. It was amazing. You could build rafts and play in the sides of it's banks for hours. The banks of the river were composed of clay. What more could a kid want!!? Mud that you could make things with.

I spent hours scooping out mounds of clay and made sculptures of people, animals and little bowls. I left them in the sun to dry as it was hot! and in a couple of hours they were dry.

Now, I know you must be thinking, how did you get away with this for two weeks? I know! Thats the crazy thing. Beauty, it turns out never had the heart to tell my parents, that I was not going to school. Also, I think she knew that she would get fired. Which is what happened once it had all came to light.

So, in the afternoon I waited for the sound of the land rover as it approached our house and then I would begin the long journey home. It wasn't a very long journey home, but it sure felt like it to me. Why? It was time to face the music.

Even just the thought of going home was enough to scare the living daylights out of me, but the thought of spending the night out in the bush-veld was even more scary for me. So I made my way back to the house, and climbed over the wall and into the house.

Suddenly Beauty was not so beautiful! In fact she had transformed into this monster who screamed at me at the top of her voice and in another language which I did not need to understand. I got the gist of it.

In short I was in for some big trouble, when my folks got home. She ranted and raved at me for a while and then got me cleaned up for when my parents got home.

Then there was the wait and the torture of knowing that soon I was going to be in big trouble and have a very sore backside. I listened for the sound of the car as it came towards the house.

Then I heard it and it was only a matter of time before Beauty, told my parents about my little adventure earlier that day.

I heard them coming in the door, and I braced myself for what was about to happen. I was as ready as I was ever going to be.

In they walked and Beauty I was sure was about to bring a whole heap of pain my way.

My mom was the first to speak and asked how the day went. To which Beauty replied. " everything went well madam, the children are ready for bed."

My heart nearly stopped. I was flooded with relief that I would be going to bed with a pain free bum.

Chapter 4
WHEN HAGAR THE HORRIBLE
CAME HOME.

Growing up in our crazy home, was a bit like growing up in the times of the vikings. It was a very male dominated household. My dad had a favourite newspaper cartoon strip called <u>Hagar the horrible!</u>

The character was a portly Viking chief with shoulder length hair and a long beard. He was in fact a bit of a party animal who liked a good fight from time to time. In other words he was just like my dad!

My dad was not averse to going to a pub and by the time he had left all hell had broken loose with fists flying and glass had been broken..

Yep, my dad was a modern day version of Hagar the horrible.

He even resembled the character, in that he had the same big belly, hairdo and beard.

If you dressed him in the same clothes as the cartoon character, then he would be a real life version of Hagar!

I remember one morning I made my way
to the living room of our house, and was
shocked to see my dad fast asleep on
the floor. It turned out he had come
home rather late at night after one of his
pub crawls.

How he even managed to drive his car home was beyond me! He was so drunk that when he got home he thought that the large brown rug on our living room floor was a blanket.

It seemed that he had kicked his shoes off and had climbed straight under the rug, and had gone to sleep with only his bearded head visible.

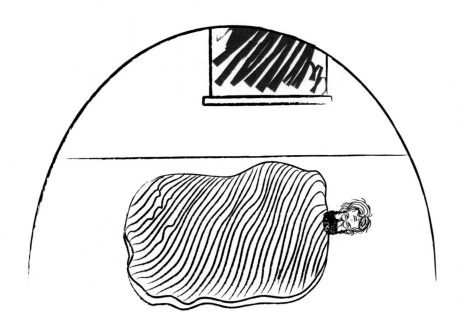

This was what greeted me when I walked into the living room. I have to say that at first, I was quite shocked as I did not know who or what was under our rug in the living room.

All manner of thoughts ran through my head as I edged closer to the rug and recognised the face of my dad, who was still sound asleep and snoring away totally oblivious to where he was.

I quickly went and got my mom and sister who thought that this was hilarious, and a little disturbing. My mom tried to wake him up, but gave up as he was so sound asleep.

Now what did this have to do with Hagar the horrible? Well, it was a few years later that my grandmother sent us a letter.

In it was a cartoon strip of Hagar the horrible that she had cut out and sent to us.

It was totally my dad. In this cartoon strip Hagar had arrived home so drunk and had not wanted to wake his wife who would have gone nuts had she seen him! He had, instead crawled under a bear skin rug in the living room and had gone to sleep.

In the morning his family found had him fast asleep under the rug and were unable to wake him up.

That was why my dad's mum sent us the cartoon! After we opened it we laughed our heads off. When my dad tried to deny that it had ever happened we laughed even more!

My dad was a real life version of Hagar The Horrible!

Chapter 5
THEN THERE WAS LUCKY

Ahh Lucky! That word always warms my heart when I think about one of the most insane and lovable dogs, that we had the great fortune to have in our lives.

Lucky was a breed of dog in South Africa that was bred as a guard dog due to their very intimidating nature and looks. The breed was known as a Boerbull.

A Boerbull was a cross breed between a Boxer and a Bull Mastiff. The result was what looked like a giant boxer dog with a huge head and set of jaws to match.

Lucky was one of the largest Boerbull dogs of his kind. He made people think twice before entering our garden. Just his presence was enough to put the fear of God into most who had met him.

He was a fierce looking creature and people were wise to have been afraid of him.

He had a habit of watching people who came to our house. He would assess them, and if they failed his test they were chased, screaming down the road. If he caught them they would usually end up with the rear of their pants torn to shreds.

No matter what we did to try to stop him, we where unable to stop him from doing this on a regular basis. He would do it to the poor post man
and our poor milkman.

The end result was that my dad had to fork out an a few occasions, for new uniforms. The one that broke the camels back, was when Lucky decided that he did not like the look of the milkman, and chased him all over our back garden, and over the wall.

The milkman ran to his milk float, and jumped in, and set off as fast as it could go.

The only problem with that plan was that a milk float did not have any side doors, and before he knew what was happening he was joined by Lucky, who had jumped into the passenger seat right next to him. He then proceeded to have a go at the poor man.

Well, the next thing that happened, was that the man jumped right out of the float as it was going down the hill. He sped off in the opposite direction, while Lucky sat there wondering what had happened to the milk man as it ploughed into a garden wall at the bottom of the hill.

That cost my dad a great deal of money for the repairs. It was shortly after that, that my dad found a new home for Lucky. I was heart broken. I always felt totally safe with Lucky by my side.

I was his favourite person in our family, and God help anyone who raised there voice against me or showed me any kind of aggression.

That would be the last time that they ever did that.

Lucky was incredibly protective of me. For this I was grateful especially when my father tried to discipline me, which was on a regular basis due to my bad behaviour and my dads drinking habit.

When my dad came home after a night out at the pub, Lucky would immediately stand between him and me and let my dad know in no uncertain terms that it would be best for him to go to bed and sleep it off.

There were a few times that my dad decided to ignore the warning and boy did he pay the price.

Lucky was a huge beast of a dog and if he felt that my dad was in any way a threat to me, or our family he would launch right into my dad, and all hell would break loose. It was so bizarre watching a fight between a drunk man and a huge dog.

My dad, in his drunken state, thought he could handle Lucky. He was sorely mistaken and there were howls of pain and bits of clothing, furniture, lamps and fragments of ornaments flying through the air as well as my dads choice words of displeasure.

I wondered what the neighbours must have thought. It was a very different time, from our present politically correct day.

It would be in the morning that my dad would realise that he had lost yet another fight with the dog! He would wake up and the pain from the puncture wounds in his arms and legs would alert him to the fact, that he had been on the wrong side of Lucky.

I would have loved to have been a fly on the wall at his work place, when he had tried to explain to his work mates why his hands were all bandaged up, and that he could barely sit down due to the wounds in his legs and behind.

Suffice it to say, that Lucky saved me from my fair share of spankings, while he lived with us. I loved him above all of our dogs, that we had over the years. I can't explain it, but we had this incredible bond between us.

Unfortunately for me the day came when we said our goodbyes to Lucky

I was heart broken to see him go and how I wished all be it for selfish reasons, that he had never chased the milkman.

Chapter 6
THE MISSING BITS.

Looking For the Little People.

Another huge cultural difference is that in the 70s up until 1976 it was illegal to own a T.V. In South Africa.

This meant that in the evenings instead of watching TV. we would sit in the living room and listen to the radio. My favourite programs were Jet Jungle. Squad cars. the Men from the Ministry and the Navy Lark.

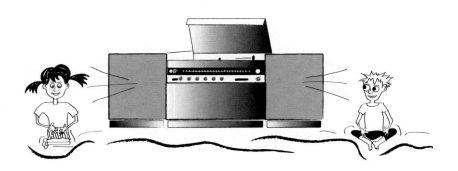

As a six and a half year old I was a very curious child and was amazed at how people managed to get inside of the speakers of my dads hi fi. After a few months of listening to them, I could not resist the temptation to find these tiny people inside the speakers.

So after I had found my dads toolbox and had managed to take his speakers apart and had gotten the last screw out of the back of the first speaker. I was so excited to see who and what was inside! I had opened it and to my surprise there was nothing but a bunch of wires and and speakers.

So I thought, maybe they were in the other speaker. So I had unscrewed the back and was all excited to finally meet them. But no, it was just the same as the other one. So just to be thorough I dismantled the speakers completely.

It was then that I realised that I would need to put this mess of wires and bits and pieces of electrical components back together.

All I can say is that I gave it my best shot and managed to get the speakers to look like they did before. Seemed good to me, except for the handful of electrical components that did not seem to fit anywhere inside the speakers.
So what was I to do?

It was obvious to me that they were not essential, so I threw them into the bin and carried on with my day with a feeling of confusion and disappointment at not finding the little people inside.

Needless to say— That evening when it came to our entertainment. I unfortunately became the evenings entertainment after my father could not get the hi fi to work.

It switched on but no sound came from the speakers. It was then that I realised that those pieces of electrical bits might have have something to do with it, and now they were in the bin somewhere.

My dad who was a very practical kind of man and an engineer to boot, decided to check the speakers for himself.

I almost felt like telling him that there was nobody inside the speakers as I had already checked earlier that morning.

When my dad took the first speaker apart I knew that this was going to mean trouble for me.

My dad took one look inside and then looked straight at me. I tried my best to look innocent, but it obviously did not work.

My dad gave me the look that meant I was in big trouble and then proceeded to open the back of the other speaker.

The look on my dads face made me get up and I started running for cover and I had thoughts of where are my comics? I needed them as padding for my butt as I knew this was going to be painful! and I was right.

Not only did I get a sore butt, but I was covered in stinky and sticky garbage. I had sifted through the bin looking for all the missing parts until I had found them all.

My dad was able to fix the speakers and the little people came back to entertain us.

There was another time when I was not so fortunate. I was not able to find all the missing bits that I had thrown away.

My First and Last Motorbike.

I remember the day my Dad came home with this amazing present. It was in the 70's and they had just started to sell these electric kids motorbikes.

Nowadays you can buy them for less than a hundred pounds, but then they cost hundreds of pounds.

My dad bought me one and I was so happy that I could go outside and show it off in front of the other kids.

However... My curiosity had gotten the better of me and I had decided that I wanted to see how this thing worked, and the only way I found that out was that I had to dismantle it and so it was that I found my dad's toolbox and then the problems started.

I took the motor apart, and then tried to put it back together. Big mistake! As in the past episode I had spare bits and what did I do. You guessed it. I threw them away in the bin.

Then I hid the bike in the cupboard and it never saw the light of day for at least six months. For that period of time I was safe from the wrath of my Dad.

But that all changed when my parents informed us that we would be moving to a new house with a nice big garden and a paved driveway and that that would be great for the motorbike.

You could have imagined my excitement! Not. I then realised that the parts were long gone and my dad was going to find out about the bike and that I was going to need those comics again.

So when we had moved and arrived at the new house one of the first things my dad wanted to do was to try the bike out on the new driveway. I will leave the rest to your imagination. Suffice it to say that I was unable to sit properly for a good few days.

Needless to say that after that episode, my dad was not very keen to buy me anything that was electronic, incase I decided to find out how it worked.

And when I had tried to get him to allow me to get a proper motor bike. He thought it was hilarious. I have never had another motorbike of any kind since then.

DURBAN 1974 to 76

Chapter 7
HAVE YOU SEEN MA TEEF?

Ahh! parents and their parties could be quite embarrassing!

I remember one such party when the booze was flowing, and the music was blaring. All these adults were giving us kids great entertainment, as they danced and made absolute fools — as we saw it — of themselves.

These parties were common when we were growing up and left me with some outstanding and fond memories.

This is one of those memories.

The year was 1975. It was a hot summers night in Sutton Park, one of the suburbs of Durban, in South Africa.

The party was jumping, the beer was flowing and everyone was, let's just put it this way well and truly over the drink and drive limit.

It seemed to go on all night and we loved it as they were usually too drunk to put us to bed. Hey! we weren't complaining. Eventually as the night drew on we all fell asleep, and only woke up on the Saturday morning.

The house was quiet and no one was going to be up for a while, so we just helped ourselves to breakfast and got on with the day until people started to wake up.

The first person that woke up was my mom. She seemed to have lost something, and was searching all over the house for whatever she had lost.

Eventually after looking all over the place she came to my sister and I, and asked, "have yoo seen ma teeff?".

After having a chuckle to ourselves we answered that we did not know where they where.

My mom had falsers, and had somehow lost them during the party. She was freaking out trying to find them.

You had to be there to appreciate the sight of a well and truly hungover person that was trying to get a shred of dignity, by trying to find her missing teeth.

Ahh the memories of childhood!

Anyway the morning wore on and my mom could not find them anywhere. She did however remember to remind me to brush my teeth or I would end up like her. So off I went to the bathroom to brush my teeth, and to my horror, there in the basin was a set of false teeth who were smiling back at me.

It turned out that my mom had felt sick during the party, and had vomited into the basin, but did not have any memory of it at all.

I was eventually able to tell my mom
(after showing my sister.) and having a
good laugh about it. that I had seen her
teeff!

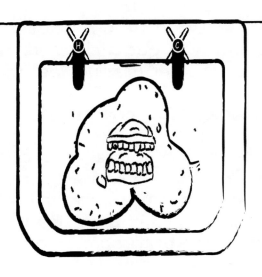

Chapter 8
CRAZY BEACH DAYS.

One of my favourite things that I did on a Saturday morning was to go to Addington beach in Durban.

It was on one of these Saturday outings that I was swept out to sea in a rip current.
This is the story of that day.

Addington beach was an amazing place to be you were a young kid.

It had a brilliant promenade with shops, rides, an amazing sea life centre, and of course the main attraction was the beach itself.

The beach with its fine golden sands stretched for miles. The water was from the Indian ocean, and as such was always at least 20 degrees centigrade in temperature. But the best part were the waves! They were amazing if you enjoyed surfing, boogie boarding, paddle ski-ing or body surfing.

I loved them all. In fact I loved the water so much that it was often the case that when we got there I would grab my boogie board, flippers and disappear for hours. I would spend the whole time catching wave after wave until I ran out of energy.

In fact to me this was one of the closest things to paradise, except for a few small wrinkles. Well not all of them were so small of a wrinkle.

There were three main culprits capable of spoiling a day in the water.

The first was what we called blue bottles.
Not the blue bottle flies that you may be picturing in your mind, but rather a very nasty little thing that was capable of inflicting great pain to any individual that was unfortunate enough to come into contact with one of these creatures.

You may know them as a Portuguese man of war. These creatures are related to the jelly fish family and they float on top of the water with a blue air sack that sits on top of the water.

When they floated and bobbed on the top of the water they looked harmless enough and even quite cute.

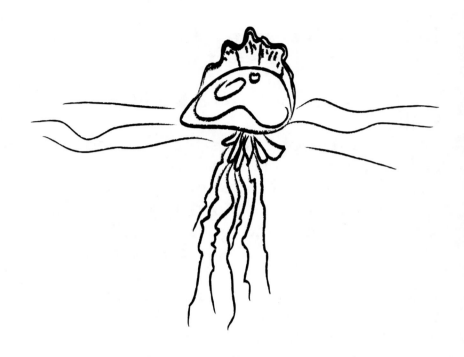

Don't let that fool you. Lying just under the surface of the water were long blue tentacles, often over a meter long. If they came into contact with your naked flesh, you would never forget your encounter with them.

I remember clearly the first time I ever came into contact with one of those creatures.
Well to be more accurate I did not come into contact with one of them, rather it was a whole group of them all at the same time.

We arrived at the beach and it was a rather windy day. I did not notice that there were not many people in the water. All I wanted to do was get into the water. The waves looked really big and perfect for boogie boarding.

On hind sight I wished that I had paid more attention to my immediate surroundings before I had run headlong into the water, and dived straight into a huge wave.

As I dived into the wave I knew that I would resurface on the other side of it. This all went to plan, but as I started to surface I felt a strange sensation all over my body.

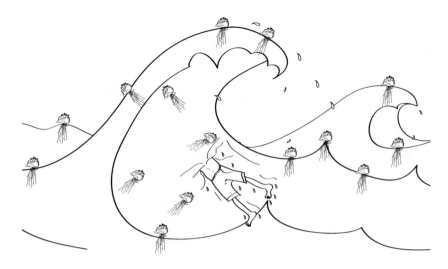

At first it felt like pins and needles, and before I could figure out why, the sensation went from pins and needles to hot and fiery pain all over my arms, legs, chest, back and face.

It turned out that there was a very good reason for there not being many people in the water. If I had taken the time to look around, I would have seen the warning sign that the lifeguards had put out, warning us that there were blue bottles in the water and that it was not safe to go into the water.

When I came screaming and running out of the water with welts all over my face and body, the life guards had the vinegar ready and doused my body. You would have thought that the vinegar would have made it worse, but in fact it did the opposite. It took the pain away.

It turned out that I had dived right into dozens of them at once, and boy had I paid the price.

That was the last time that I ran into the water without checking to see if there was any danger.

After that incident, whenever there were blue bottles on the beach I made a point of going to the waters edge and popped as many of the blighters as I could, with the heel of my foot. This was a common sight on the beach when they were there. Probably because many of those children and adults had also been stung and they were getting their revenge just like me.

The second culprit was the jelly fish itself. These were quite dangerous and on one occasion we witnessed a man that had been rather foolish. He had found a rather large jelly fish washed up on the shore. He thought that it was dead and had placed it on his head as a hat. Unfortunately for him it was one of the dumbest things he had ever done.

The jelly fish was not dead at all and was one of the more toxic and deadly ones that had been found in those waters.

The third culprit was the Great White shark.
This one was more common than the other two. In order to protect the people in the water the authorities had placed shark nets in the bay.

One of the problems with such warm water was that it attracted a great deal of sea life, and one of those was the great white shark.
For the most part we were protected from those fearsome creatures.

The bay had shark nets that had been put in place. However that was not a guarantee that sharks were not able to get through to the bathers, as we found out on more than one occasion.

It was not uncommon to arrive at the beach and find that no one was in the water, and that there had been a sighting of a shark in the water by one of the bathers or surfers. On more than one occasion we would arrive at the beach to find a huge shark surrounded by a crowd of beach goers.

Once you caught sight of that creature you did not want to go back into the water, even when the lifeguards gave the all clear.

I had always wondered how they had gotten through the nets. In my mind I had visualised a very long net, that had gone from one side of the bay to the other and had stopped the sharks from getting through to the bathers.

I thought that maybe the net had had holes and needed to be repaired, and that was how the sharks had gotten through, but that was not the case.

It turned out that was not how the shark nets worked. In fact they did not go from one side to the other. No, they were dotted in the bay. The nets were attached to floats and dangled in the water.

Fish swam into them and got caught and as they struggled to get free their vibrations were picked up by the sharks, who then made their way to the source and got caught in the nets and so it went on.

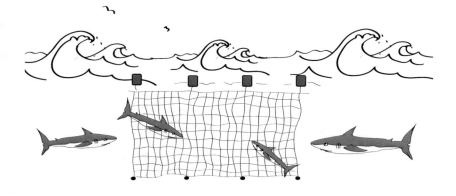

The principle was that the vibrations would be stronger near the nets than near the bathers in the waters by the shore. However some sharks headed for the vibrations made by people thrashing about in the water. To the sharks the thrashing people were like fish in distress. There were times that the sharks ended up stranded on the beach.

It was on one of these Saturday outings to the beach, that I was in the water and had paddled out over the breaking waves. I had not made a good decision, and was about to find out what it was like to get close to a shark net.

That day there was a particularly strong rip current and yes you guessed it. I got caught in it.

The thing about a rip current is that you don't know that you are in it before its too late. I had paddled out past the breakers and had suddenly realised that I was not facing the shore anymore.

If I had been facing the shore I would have noticed that the buildings were shrinking in size at a rapid pace. Instead I had been looking out to sea for the next set of swells and had been trying to figure which one I was going to catch.

I had seen one and had turned around to face the shore. I paddled in order to catch the next wave. It was then that I realised that I was much further from the shore than I had realised, and that it was getting further away by the second even though I had been paddling towards it with all my strength. It just kept getting smaller and smaller.

It was then that I realised that I was in deep deep trouble, and that I was not going to be able to get back to the shore. No matter how much I swam or paddled, I was still moving further out to sea at a rapid speed. This was my introduction to a rip current, and I did not like it one bit. I thought that I was going to die that day.

I had gotten further and further away from the shore and had become aware of a line of floats that were in the water. I had gotten close to them. I had thought to myself that I could have grabbed onto them and kept myself from drifting out further.

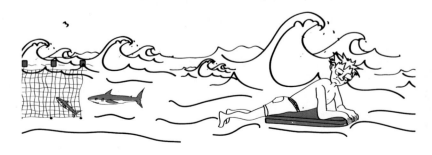

It was then thatI I heard a voice calling out to me. It was one of the life guards on his way to rescue me.

Relief had flooded my entire body, and as I waited he drew close to me and then He pulled up to me on his board, and pulled a tired boy onto it and headed back towards the shore.
I did not know it at the time, but he had saved me, not only from being dragged far out to sea and drowning, but also from the sharks. If I had made it to the floats, I would have been hanging onto the top of the shark nets and that would have probably been the end of me.

When the lifeguard pointed this out to me, I realised I was so close to the shark nets and could easily have become a snack for one of those great whites if he had not reached me in time!

Chapter 9
WHEELCHAIR RACING.

1975, not long after one of those crazy parties when we lived in Sutton Park Durban, I was playing football in the back courtyard of the block of flats we lived in.

It was an enclosed area that we could play in and be safe from strangers. The caretaker had tortoises, and he had a marmoset in a cage that he had built up against one of the walls. We used to have fun playing there and getting our fingers bitten by the marmoset's or getting peed on by a tortoise when we picked it up.

It was on a Saturday morning that I decided to go out into the courtyard to kick a football off the wall. While doing this I managed to kick the ball up onto a roof of one of the buildings on the other side of the courtyard wall.

This was not a problem as it had happened to me before and I was able to climb up from our side and onto the roof to retrieve it.

The roof was made of corrugated iron sheets, and was not the most stable of surfaces to walk on, as when you took a step the iron would give a little under your weight, and if it was rusty you could even find your foot going through the tin roof.

My ball had settled in the gutter close to the wall, that separated the two properties from one-another. The gutter was made of asbestos and as I was about to find out, it was not a very strong material. When I bent down to pick up my ball I made a mistake, that would have major consequences for me in the years to come.

The Mistake I made was that I stepped onto the gutter and placed my weight on the asbestos. Although it looked like it was strong I was about to find out that it was anything but

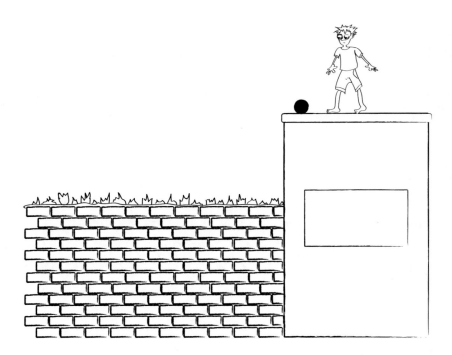

As I put my foot on it. It gave way and I was falling off the roof.

As it happens the fall would not have been that bad. as there was a large mound of sand at the bottom of the wall. and it would have broken my fall. I say would have for a very good reason.

As I started to fall my instinct was to grab for the wall just below me to stop my fall.

I was successful and landed on the wall. The problem was that I had not realised that the wall had been burglar proofed with broken glass bottles, that had been cemented onto the top of the wall.

I soon discovered as my hands and body were sliced open, and the searing pain began to course through my body, that something was very wrong!

Shortly after the pain, I noticed the blood squirting from my right hand, elbow, waist and my right leg. The razor sharp glass had ripped through the right side of my body as I fell. I quickly let go of the wall, and fell into the sand pit below and the blood just kept pouring out of my wounds.

I looked at my right hand, and began to scream, as there was no skin or flesh left on the bottom of my right index finger. It was stuck to a piece of glass on the top of the wall. In fact I could see the bone, and above it was a piece of skin and flesh just flapping about, as I ran screaming towards our flat. All the while there was a constant stream of blood flowing from my wounds.

I got to our front door and my mom could hear that there was something very wrong. She opened the door, and took one look at me and pulled me inside.

She called my dad and he came, and as soon as he saw me he grabbed me, wrapped a cloth around my right arm as my mom tried to stop the flow of blood on my leg and waist.

He picked me up and they put me straight into our VW van and broke all the speed limits as he hurtled towards Addington hospital in Durban. He did not bother with the protocols of the hospital, and just rushed through the queue and straight to a doctor who took one look at me and had me placed on a table.

He immediately started to clean the wounds and stitch them up. First my leg and waist, and then onto the more serious of my injuries, on my right elbow and then the worst, my finger and hand.

For me it was all a very frightening experience and I knew that I was going to have lots of pain in the days ahead.

Once the doctor got to my hand, and managed to get the cloth off of my hand, he realised that the injury to my index finger was very bad. There was no flesh or skin on the under side of the finger, and he had to pull the flap of skin back over the bone and stretch it over the finger to stitch it closed.

This he did, but due to the lack of skin, it meant that I was unable to straighten my finger, because there was no give from the skin, that had been stretched over my bone. The doctor informed my dad that this was a temporary solution, and that as my hands would grow, I would need further operations and skin grafts in order for my finger to be straightened.

This brings me to the wheelchair race. A year later after my finger had had a chance to heal I was in hospital for a skin graft operation. I had been there for over one month, and like any kid I was bored.

I had however, made friends with a girl who was similar in age to me. We became partners in crime as we were there together for three months. She had suffered major burns, and was having to have skin grafts as well.

One afternoon after lunch, we were bored and looking for some adventure. We were walking through the wards and we came upon a couple of wheelchairs. We both looked at each other and with a cheeky grin on our faces and jumped into a wheelchair and began to race down the halls of the hospital.

We found a hall that had a gentle decline, and was relatively quiet. This would allow us to have a decent race against each other. Both of us had bandages on our arms and we were not supposed to lower our arms so that there would not be a build up of blood pressure from our wounds.

We were too bored to pay any attention to this. We had a fantastic time racing up and down the hallway of one of the wards until an orderly caught us and sent us packing, back to our ward.

CATO RIDGE 1976 to 77

Chapter10
NO ANGEL!

In the first chapters of this book you would have got a glimpse of what I, as a child thought of school.

Well as a kid who hated school, it would probably have come as no surprise that I got up to my fair share of mischief. I think it is fair to say that I was never going to be a model student, unless there was an award for the kid who spent a great deal of time at the headmasters getting six of the best.

I remember one time, when I had been sick and in hospital for a few months and then went back to school.

In South Africa in the seventies there was a strict dress code for both boys and girls. Part of the code was that boys were not allowed to

have hair that touched their shoulders
and a fringe that reached the eyebrows.
In fact the boys were all meant to have
short back and sides.

Well after being in the hospital for 3 months, my hair had grown, and I was sent to school before getting a haircut.

I often wonder what my parents were thinking half the time. They were so busy with work and parties, that they did not always take the best of care of us kids.

That was one of those occasions when I wish they had sent me to the barbers.

It did not take long for the taunts to start, and that was from the teachers.

They started to mock my long hair and make a fool of me in the class, in front of the other kids. This led to the kids taunting and teasing me, to which I responded with some choice words of displeasure.

Unfortunately I had made the mistake of using those choice words later on in the day. By that time I was thoroughly fed up and annoyed with the situation, and when a teacher started to mock my hair do, I responded as I had with the other kids that day.

So this teacher, lets call him "Sir Paininthebutt."

He noticed my hair as soon as I entered his class, and almost immediately he started to mock me and called me a girl with my new hairdo. Without even thinking, I just responded as I had been doing with the other kids that day.

I have my parents and their friends to thank for what came out of my mouth next. So it was not really my fault, that I was sent to headmasters office for six of the best.

Anyway picture the scene. There I was being embarrassed in front of the whole class for the fifth or sixth time that day. I had just exploded with the choice words of displeasure that I had picked up from my parents.

Suffice it to say, that the air turned various shades of blue. The ripple effect was immediate, and the look of horror on Sir Paininthebutt told me all that I needed to know.

Oh how I wished that I had had. my comics with me that day. I was dragged off by my ear to the headmasters office with great speed.

Suffice it to say that I was unable to sit at the table and enjoy my dinner that night without a great deal of discomfort.

Another event that has stuck with me over the years is the time, that I stole a bike from the school. It's not one that I am proud of.

I just want to say that it would never have happened if my mom had not fed me some dodgy food that morning for breakfast.

Oh let me just say that if you are of a sensitive nature or are easily offended then you might want to skip to the next chapter.

It happened like this.
One day while we on one our lunch break, and as you do when you are a kid, you have times when you are trying to impress a member of the opposite sex. We were showing the girls just how brave and manly we were by climbing trees with the greatest of ease.

As all the boys knew, this is one of the best ways to impress a girl that you liked. Part of the way to impress, was to be the first to get to the top of the tree. It was a kind of a show of strength and ability. It was also a race between the boys.

On this occasion, I had managed to scramble past the other boys and was climbing the tree with ease.

I was at least half way up the tree with another boy just below me. It was then, that I felt the rumble in my tummy. I didn't think much of it at the time, other than the thought of how this could work to my advantage.

To me it had the familiar feel of a huge fart about to be let loose. My plan was to let the kid below get right up close, and then let him have it as I scarpered up to the top of the tree. Oh man this was going to be good!

Or so I thought. In fact it was going to be good, but not for me. It was going to be a great source of hilarity for all the other kids who were watching what was going on up the tree.

Closer, just a little bit more, closer and then Bammm! I let it loose and at first the smell was awful! Yes!

Success, I had done a complete stinker that would send the kid below me down the tree. Well that is exactly what happened.

He took one look at me and his face had an expression of total disgust. I thought to myself, that will teach you to compete with me.

However I started to feel a strange sensation on my legs. It felt kind of squishy in my shorts and there was a sensation of something running down my legs.

It almost felt like liquid, but that could not be.

So I took a quick peek to see what was going on and to my horror, my legs did indeed have liquid running down them.

The problem was that it was lumpy yellowy brown and rather putrid smelling.

Yes you may have guessed it by now that my victorious fart was in fact what I would come to know to be a wet one!

It turned out that I had a case of the runs, and boy was it running, all the way down my legs.

The people below started to point towards me and started to laugh, and move out from under the tree just incase some landed on them.

I have to say that I have never been more embarrassed in my life, and I knew that I would now be the laughing stock of the playground as well as the entire school.

I made my way down the tree and made a hasty exit from the playground to the back of the school, where I thought that there would be less people.

It turned out that I was right. I was desperate to get home, but the problem was that it was at least five miles away, and I was not going to be able to walk with this goo all over my legs.

By now, it had started to dry in the heat and had stuck to my legs. It was a most uncomfortable sensation.

It turned out that at the back of the school was where the kids would parked their bikes. I was so desperate to get home that I hatched the plan to steal one of those bikes.

I was all of seven years old at the time, and about to steal my first and last bike.

I went through the bike racks until I found one that was not locked or chained to the rack. It was perfect for me and I took it and made my way home as fast as my little, and by now, crusty legs could go.

When I eventually got home in the stifling afternoon heat, my legs were totally encrusted with that goo and the flies were loving it as they swarmed around me.

I rode down our driveway and looked for a place to hide the bike. Eventually I came across my dad's little three wheeler, tuk tuk and hid it in the back of it. Believing that no one had seen me, I went into the house and ran a bath.

It turned out I had not escaped unseen with the bike and in the morning there was a man at our door looking for his son's bike.

Yepp, you guessed it I needed the comics again!!

Chapter11
THE FLYING TERMITES & OTHER INSECTS.

Boom, boom, boom, boom, boom and boom. Six loud explosions one after the other shattered the peace of a Saturday afternoon in the African bush as it started raining clumps of red earth and little white termites!

What was I doing? I was running for cover.

Growing up in a subtropical climate meant that we had a vast variety of insects.

We had all kinds of ants, termites, spiders, cockroaches, huge ticks and flying insects.

I need to say that if you don't like insects then Africa is not the place for you! As for me I never really had any phobia's about them. Except for the spiders. Oh man! The spiders were huge. They were the size of a young child's hand.

Imagine going to sleep and then waking up in the morning and looking up at your ceiling and there above your head is this massive and often very colourful spider calmly looking down at you.

The mind boggles when as a 9 year old, you thought to yourself that there was no sign of it before you went to bed, and now there it was and how did it get in? Also what was it doing while you were sleeping? I still get the hee bee gee bees when I think about it.

Anyway Im getting distracted.

I remember the day I discovered thunderflashes. It was guy faulks in the seventies, and there were no health and safety regulations in those days. A child could go to the corner cafe and buy all kinds of fireworks.

There were rockets, spinners, catherine wheels, bangers and my personal favourite, the thunder flash.

That was the big daddy of them all! It resembled a stick of dynamite except that it was only two thirds, the size of a stick of dynamite.

They were incredibly loud and, yes very dangerous. If one had gone off in your hands, it was quite likely that you would loose at least a couple of fingers.

To this day I am still amazed that I have all my fingers, and both eyes. I almost lost my finger and hand, but that had nothing to do with thunderflashes and that is for another story.

Anyway, back to the thunderflashes and how they made the termites fly. One of the problems that a farmer did face in South Africa was termites, and their huge mounds that housed their colonies. These to me looked almost like miniature volcanoes.

They rose out of the ground and would often be well over six feet tall, four or five feet wide and made of red earth. They were huge and incredibly strong and had been known to wreck the odd vehicle that drove though the bush.

These mounds were full of termites. They were large white termites that were capable of destroying your crops of wheat, and grasses. They would eat your wooden fence posts, and buildings. They where a huge pest for the farmers.

They were very hard to eradicate. I can tell you from experience, that if they had bitten you, you would not easily have forgotten it. I remember the first time I stumbled into one of those termite mounds when I was out on one of my many adventures in the bush.

I was fascinated with this huge red
volcano looking mound, and decided to
climb up it to have a look inside it from
the top. Well I can tell you that, that
was a big mistake as they were very
defensive of their mounds, and before I
got to the top, I started to feel their
wrath.

Man, those things could bite. The army
termites had huge talons that released
some kind of toxin when they bit you, and
wow I really got hurt.

It did not take me long to jump off of the mound, but by then I was covered in these termites and getting bitten all over. The only upside to them is, that they are quite soft and can be easily squished as you brush them off.

So what did this have to do with thunderflashes?

Well in one word, REVENGE! I was going to sort them out. I knew that they were a pest and that they were very destructive and now it was my turn to try and have them eradicted. Thats where the thunderflashes came in handy.

I went and counted my pocket money and realised that I had enough to buy at least 6 of them. So off I trotted to the shop, bought them and then I made plans to blow the termites to kingdom come.

I know, it sounds awful and very politically incorrect, but it's what happened and you need to understand that we did not have any sympathy for termites, and I think that anyone who has had to deal with those insects would not have had much sympathy for them either.

However, that did not mean that what I did was a good thing. In fact it was a very stupid and dangerous thing to do. That's why I did it! I liked danger and I was often very stupid and amazingly still alive to tell the story.

So this is how it went down. I got a big stick and sharpened the end with my knife. Yes I had a knife, and I carried it with me everywhere, as did most boys in South Africa. We all had pen knives of varying sizes.

So with my stick sharpened, a box of matches, and my pockets bulging with thunder flashes,

I approached the mound and started to gouge holes into the base of the mound. Six holes later, and quite a lot of angry termites biting into the wood as if to kill it while making their way up my stick, I was ready to place the thunder flashes into the holes I had made.

I knew that I would need to be quick as the termites would swarm over the explosives, and were quite capable of biting through the wick. I shoved them in, and lit them as quickly as I could and waited for the loud bangs as they would go off.

I ran a short distance, and watched as one by one, they exploded with a few seconds between each explosion.

What a mess was made that day. Bits of the mound were flying everywhere, and so where the termites. They flew much higher and further than I had anticipated and yes, you guessed it right towards me!

In the end I was covered in red earth and bits of termites as well as some very aggravated termites who were letting me know that they were not at all happy with what had just happened.

However, once the dust had settled and I was able to view my handiwork, I was pleased with the results, and willing to endure the pain of a few termites digging into my flesh.

I went away satisfied in the knowledge that I had done a good job of ridding my father of one of our biggest pests. However It was short lived, as a few weeks later when I returned where the mound had once been there was a brand new mound in its place. I stood there scratching my head in astonishment at how quickly they had managed to build a brand new one!

Chapter12
TAKEN FOR A RIDE.

TailStar had been galloping at full speed up our driveway and I had been holding on for dear life. Screaming at the top of my lungs for him to slow down or stop, but all to no avail. No matter what I did I was not able to control him. The only thing I could do was to hold on in sheer terror and hope, that I didn't fall off and break my neck.

In an earlier chapter about the weekend parties, I spoke about my horse Tailstar. He was already sixteen years old when his owner decided to give him to me. I was 9 years old at the time.

I loved that horse. He was very friendly and we took to each other. I would groom him, feed him, and we would go on adventures together through the surrounding farmlands, and rolling lush hills of KwaZulu.

Our School was in the nearest town of Cato ridge, and we would be collected by the minibus everyday, and were dropped off at the bottom of the main dirt road in the afternoon. I would then have had to walk another three miles of dirt road just to get to our driveway which was two and a half miles long.

It was not a very pleasant walk home in the scorching heat and humidity. I always dreaded the walk home, and could not wait to get home, and out of my school uniform, and shoes. When I was given Tailstar, things changed for the better when it came to my walk home.

Tailstar was a very friendly horse and was allowed to roam through the fields, that would go all the way down to the bottom of our fence, which bordered the dirt road, that I had to walk along every afternoon after school.

One afternoon, shortly after TailStar arrived, I was beginning my walk home after being dropped off by the minibus.

I had walked about half a mile, when out
of the bush this horse appeared.

It was TailStar, and he immediately
trotted over to the fence and allowed me
to stroke him.

It was then, that I had a brain wave and
wondered if he would allow me to mount
him bareback, and take me home.

If this worked, it would save me a very long and uncomfortable walk home everyday.

The problem was, that I would not be able to mount him without pulling on his mane, and from previous experience I knew that, that would be out of the question.

I looked around, and realised that the fence posts were just the right height for me to climb onto his back. The posts were made of thick tree trunks, and were wide enough for me to stand on.

I called TailStar over to the post and I climbed up onto the top of a fence post, so that I would have the height to be able to step over his back and mount him with ease.

I waited till he was lined up, and tried to mount him. It worked and he did not seem to mind at all. What a relief.

From that day onwards TailStar would make his way down to the fence at the exact time that I would be dropped off after school. We would greet each other, and after I had mounted him, we would take a slow stroll up to the house.

I felt like a cool cowboy, and learnt how to ride Tailstar without a saddle.

It was like two friends getting together to hang out. We looked forward to seeing each other every day.

He was a friendly horse, who for the most part was very easy going. However, sometimes he was like a completely different horse to the one I have just described.

Now back to me, who had been screaming for my life, as he galloped at full speed up our driveway.

It was a beautiful Saturday morning, the sun was splitting the trees and I felt like an adventure.

I thought that I would maybe go to the dam and build a raft, or climb some hills in the distance, or go to the tiny farm shop for sweets on a farm six miles away.

I had decided to go for a day out with TailStar. I went to the stable, and saddled him up and took some water with me.

I was looking forward to a great day of adventure and discovery. Boy was I going to get some adventure, just not the kind I was thinking of.

So we set off and headed on down the driveway, which meandered down a hill to the bottom entrance.

Once there, I looked at the scene before me, and decided that I wanted to head on up the hills, and yes, get to the tiny farm shop, which had a window with a coke sign above it.

It was just part of someones farmhouse, and they had found a way to make extra cash. There were no shops for at least ten miles in either direction.

So I turned right, and off we trotted up the dirt road until it got us to a smaller walking path, that would take us to the top of the hills. I loved this kind of adventure in the bush-veld of South Africa.

Anyway, so after a couple of hours of walking through the hills in stifling hot temperatures, we eventually got to where the shop was, and I bought a coke and some sweets. Then I decided that I wanted to explore the area a bit more, and started heading further into the hills.

That's when the trouble started. I found out that TailStar was not as keen as I was, to carry on exploring the area. It was becoming harder to get him to respond to my promptings and my commands.

After about ten minutes it became apparent that I was not going to get to discover more of the area we were in.

I was just about to give in to TailStar when he decided that he wanted to go home, and that was that. I would like to say, that we took a leisurely stroll home, but that is not what happened.

It was on that day, that I discovered that there was no way of stopping him, once he had decided to go home.
Imagine a 9 year old kid trying to get this powerful beast creature to do his bidding. I thought that I was the great adventurer and that he was my trusty steed. Not so!

On that day I realised that TailStar was the one in charge, and that he was only letting me have some fun until he had had enough.

Now he had, had enough, and he started out with a slow but steady trot toward our farm and once the path widened he went into a full gallop all the way home.

I could not hold onto the reigns, because once he was in full gallop he would be stretched out completely, and my small frame could not stretch all the way forward as he lunged forward at lightning pace.

I feared that I would be pulled out of my saddle, and be flung over his head and trampled underneath. By then, I was screaming in terror at the top of my voice, but all to no avail.

By now I had lost my grip on the reigns and all I could do, was grab hold of his mane, and scream and hope, for the best.

Before I knew it, I could see our driveway approaching in the distance.

A feeling of relief came over me as we turned into the driveway. I hung on for dear life. Not long now I thought. All I have to do is hold on to his mane for a little bit longer.

Half way up the driveway our Dalmatian called Wullie came bursting through the bushes, no doubt attracted by the screams that were emanating from me.

He seemed delighted to be part of this game, and proceeded to bark at TailStar and tried to nip his ankles with his teeth.

This caused TailStar to deviate from the driveway, and to run full tilt through the thorn bushes, and as you may have guessed by now, I was wearing shorts and a t shirt.

So through the bushes we went and with me screaming my head off, our dog barking his head off and TailStar had just decided that he had, had enough, and he rose up onto his back legs, and threw me though the air onto a pile of jagged rocks.

I remember the sensation of flying through the air, and then the pain of hitting the rocks.

My left leg took the brunt of the impact as my shin smashed into a rock that left a gaping hole in my leg as the blood gushed out. All this time Wullie thought that this was a funny game. I lay there crumpled into a ball as the pain shot through my leg, and I had to wait for it to subside.

I had learnt a big lesson that day about my horse. I had learnt to look out for the signs that he was getting fed up with the ride. Once he had decided that he had had enough, then it was best for me to have turned back and gone home.

Chapter13
LOTS OF SNAKES

Africa! aahh there is no place like it.
Once you go there and live there, it will
always be in your blood. Everything is so
different. The people, the noises, the
blueness of the sky, the thunder storms,
the roads, the houses, the food, the
insects and of course the wildlife.

One of the most prolific creatures in the bush-veld of KwaZulu Natal was the Snake. In fact there were so many different kinds of snakes there. It was the perfect climate for these creatures and they thrived.

We had Puff Adders galore, Wrinkals, which was a kind of Cobra, Black mambas, Green mambas, and one of the most deadly of them all the Boom Slang (Tree Snake). To name but a few of the highly toxic and life threatening snakes that were common place on our farmlands.

Despite this fact, we still just ran around in shorts and a T shirt. No shoes or anything to protect our legs from being bitten by a snake, which almost certainly would have lead to, at best, being maimed or one could even have died from a snake bite..

This never bothered me as I had been taught by our Farm worker's kids how to catch these highly venomous snakes, and how to deal with them.

Living on a remote farm meant that my closest friends were the children of the farm labourers. Those kids were hardy and knew the bush veld like the back of their hands. They were excellent hunters and fantastic snake catchers.

It was from them that I learned how to catch snakes without killing myself. This became a valued skill, especially as we had to be able to get rid of the snakes, when they would make their way into the barn, where we stabled the horses.

My job was to go in and catch them so that the horses would stop being skittish and would stop them from hurting themselves while destroying their stalls as they tried to get away from the snakes.

The trick was to catch them, without getting too close to the dangerous end of the creature?

For this, we needed a branch that we had selected from a tree. We cut it off and made sure that it had a y shape at the end of it. It had to be about a meter and a half long and needed to be strong enough to keep the snakes head pinned to the ground with the y end.

Then one reached down and grabbed the snake behind the head, and held it tight, so that it could not get it's head free to bite. That was how I cought all manner of snakes, without being bitten.

It was on one of those nights when the snakes had managed to get into the stables. I went to see what was going on, and took my stick, sure enough, there were three snakes in the barn. I caught them and they were quite aggressive, and by the looks of their fangs looked quite venomous. I placed them in a sack that I had taken with me to put them in.

That was when I had a great idea! Why had I not thought of this before? I had this really nice big fish tank. To my mind I thought it would make a wonderful home for these three snakes.

So, I put some small tree branches in it, and some rocks from the garden, and some water and placed them in the tank.

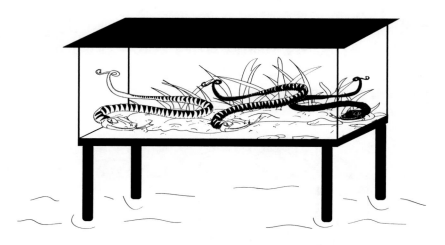

Two of the snakes were about half a meter long, while the other one was over a meter, and much thicker than the others.

I stood back and admired my new snake tank, but I forgot about one very important thing, that they would need. Food! My mom was not very happy at all, at the thought of three snakes in our home.

She was convinced that nothing good would come of this, and that I was looking for trouble. I unfortunately did not check on them for the next few days, and then came home from town only to find that the two smaller snakes had gone missing.

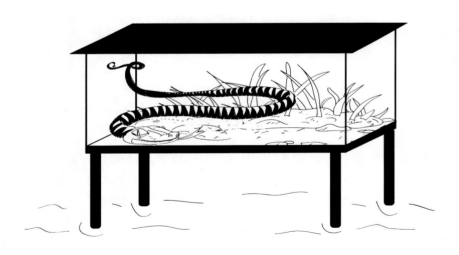

I had searched through the tank and was not able to find them anywhere, and so panic set in.

My dad was now involved and he asked me what I had been feeding them? That's when I realised that I hadn't even thought about feeding them. So my dad, after giving me a rather mean look, said that he thought that the large snake, that was still there, may have eaten the other two.

So now we had to kill this poor snake and cut it open to see if the other snakes were inside it. We found no evidence of the other snakes.

Now even more panic began to set in, as I realised that they were probably somewhere in the house, and by now my mom had become frantic as she realised what had happened. The two smaller snakes had managed to escape into our home.

Suddenly I was not that popular in our household. My dad, mom and sister were all very upset with me.

Well weeks and months went by without any trace of the snakes, and so we all forgot about them, until one day about three months later the last person that I would have wanted to find one of the snakes, did just that.

It was my Mom. Oh boy!, you should have heard the screams, and the very choice words of displeasure, that she used when she summoned me to the kitchen.

My mom had found the snake when she opened the cupboard under the kitchen sink, and while she had been rummaging around looking for a pot she had brushed against the hot water pipe, and felt the hot water pipe slither and hiss at her.

By some miracle she was not bitten. Needless to say, once again, I was not the most popular person in our home again.

I had to catch that snake and get rid of it. I did so, and took it far out into the bush and let it go. We never found the other missing snake, and in the back of our minds whenever we went to bed there was always the thought that it may have been in the house. Needless to say I was never allowed to keep any kind of snake as a pet after that fiasco.

The kids from the farm did not keep the snakes.

In fact if they caught a snake, it did not live for very long. They would pin it down by the head and then, they would grab the tail, and with one swift stroke they would whip the snake and hit its head on a nearby rock. That would usually kill it outright, then they would skin it and take it home to eat it.

On the farm we would often have fires as the summer heated things up. Our farm was surrounded by sugar cane farms, and when one of them caught alight, it did not take long for an inferno to travel across the field, and set all the surrounding fields alight.

When this happened it was all hands on deck. Every farmer, their families, and workers would jump into action to, not only save the crops, but also their property and lives of their animals.

These fires were savage, and the heat was so intense, that you could feel your skin drying out, as the heat emanated from the liquid sugar, that was igniting, due to the stifling heat. The air was so warm that it was uncomfortable breathing it in.

When these fires happened we would make a fire break, and do our best to keep the fire from spreading. One of the strange things that would happen, while we were there, is that the animals in the fields would come running out of the crops and into the firebreak in order to escape the fire.

There were rats, insects of all kinds, rabbits, dogs, cats, deer, and a variety of snakes, most of them venomous. We would do our best to save as many of the creatures as possible, except for the snakes!

This is where our compassion had it's limits.

This is also where the speed and agility of the kids on the farmlands came into it's own. They would grab these snakes, who by then were quite out of sorts and bewildered, by all that was happening.

They would grab them by the tail and swing them around above their heads to gather speed, and then let them fly right back into the heart of the fire. That would be the end of them.

I remembered the first time when my dad saw me doing the same with a highly venomous snake. He nearly collapsed with fear as I grabbed it and sent it flying back into the flames.

Needles to say he was not too impressed, as I might have been bitten and died, but I was well taught by the kids of the farm labourers. They were masters at this.

On our farm we had large sheds with concrete floors and walls. In the shed there were rows after rows of cages suspended a half meter from the floor. In them we kept our main animals that we had bred.

We farmed rabbits for their meat. We started off with 12 rabbits, and before we knew it, we had hundreds of rabbits, and yes the saying is true, they breed like rabbits!

We had over 2000 rabbits at any one time. The cages were suspended, so that rats and snakes could not get to the rabbits and their kittens.

There were many times that snakes had managed to get in, and kill the kittens and had eaten them. This usually happened at night and we would discover what had happened, in the morning. On some of the occasions when they would get in it would be daytime and we would hear the rabbits start to scream!

Yes rabbits can scream and they scream very loudly.

On one of these occasions, my mom heard the screams and went and got her gun. A point 22 pistol. She went into the shed and sure enough she found a snake trying to get into the cage to kill and eat a rabbit.

Without thinking, she sprang into action and fired every bullet in the guns magazine toward that snake. Click, click, click and no more bullets, however the snake was completely unscathed and managed to get away to fight another day.

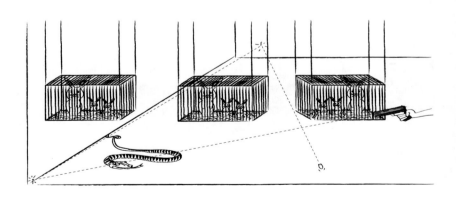

The rabbits on the other hand, were not quite as fortunate. In fact there were quite a few casualties that day. My mom, never was a great aim and did not come close to hitting the snake.

Never mind the fact, that she was in a concrete room, and the bullets had all ricocheted around the shed and killed at least half a dozen of our rabbits.

Needless to say my mom was a very practical person and that meant we had rabbit stew and rabbit curry for the next week or two.

On another occasion, I was relaxing under a tree by our duck pond. It was a beautiful morning, and I was just getting ready to get on with the day, when I felt a tap on my shoulder.

At first I thought that it was my sister playing a trick on me, and the smell hit me.

Some snakes give off a very distinctive smell, and this smell meant that there was a snake .in the tree. It was a green mamba that had decided to use my shoulder as a stepping stone to make its way to the ground from a branch in the tree.

As I sat there it slithered down my left shoulder, and into the duck pond, and out the other end.

Once I had gotten over the shock of it, I screamed to my mom that there was a snake!

My mom heard the tome in my scream and so she knew that there was a problem. before I knew it she was running out of the house with a gun in her hand.

My brave mother who was well out of her depth, ran over to where I was. I pointed to the snake which was slithering over the grass.

She chased after it and managed to corner a Green mamba! That in itself was a big mistake, as they could be very aggressive and have been known to chase people to bite them.

So my mom with the gun in her hand stood and blocked the way of escape of one of the most deadly snakes in the world. She pointed the pistol at it and pulled the trigger and click, click, click was all that one could hear!

It turned out that in her haste she had forgotten to load the magazine with into the gun. It all happened so fast.

One minute my mom was standing there like some kind of super hero that was about to vanquish her foe. The next minute there was this screaming woman who was running as fast as her legs could carry her, away from where the snake had been cornered.

All of her maternal instincts were gone in a split second, and now it was everyone for themselves.

As she sped past me I half expected to see a green streak, chasing close behind, but there was no sign of the snake. It turned out that the snake was more confused than anything else, and just sat there wondering what on earth this crazy human was doing.

It just stared at her as she was running away. It then made its way back into the long grass, never to be seen again.

Chapter 14
TRACTOR TROUBLE

As I was thinking of bees and wasps it reminded me of the time that I had managed to get hold of my dad's tractor key.

Now as a young boy I used to watch my dad out on the tractor, and being on the tractor with him made me realise that this tractor driving was easy, or so I thought. I knew from observing him that if you turned the key and put it into gear, it would go. Easy!

Well, I was to learn a big lesson that day, and I am so grateful that one of our farm labourers was there to rescue me, or there would have been serious consequences for me, the banana trees and the bees!

I made my way to the shed where the tractor was parked. It looked huge. It was on old and very heavy light grey colour.

At first I thought this was probably not such a good idea but promptly decided that this was going to be fun. I hopped up onto the seat and put the key into the ignition.

I turned the key and the thing started to rumble and shake as the engine came to life. The noise was ear shattering as there was no cab to sit in.

This was one of those pre cabin tractors so there was no protection from the noise, except for ear muffs which I did not have.

So now that it had come to life, I put it into gear and then the fun began! I grabbed hold of the gear lever with both hands, and was completely oblivious to a thing called a clutch. Somehow I managed with a lot of grinding noises to force it into one of those gears.

Suddenly it jerked forward and I grabbed the steering wheel and started to steer it down the dirt road. All seemed fine as it was now moving forward at walking pace. I thought to myself, that I had this and that this was easy and fun.

So I carried on down the dirt road,
towards the end of the track. At the end
of the track was a grove of banana trees
and behind them, the bee hives.

At first I didn't think there were going to
be any problems as this thing was easy
to control.

It had not yet occurred to me that at the
end of the track, I would need to be able
to stop the tractor, and turn it around, so
that I could put it back where I found it,
without my father finding out.

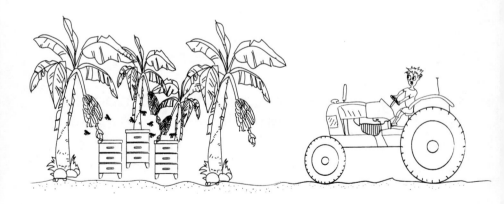

It turned out that it was easy to control as long as you were going in a relatively straight line. I discovered that while trying to turn this huge thing, while traveling at walking pace was proving to be more than my little arms could manage.

As I drew closer to the banana trees I tried to steer the tractor to the left, so that I could go around the trees, and miss the bees. At that speed, I could not get the steering wheel to go the direction I wanted it to.

I was getting closer with every second, and now the panic set in. I could see the trees just metres in front of me, so I mustered all my strength to turn this sucker and only managed to turn it slightly to the left, but nowhere near enough, to miss the banana trees and the bees!

The tractor was a golden oldie, the kind that one would see at the vintage car rallies. The kind with the cast iron seats. It was super heavy, as I was about to find out.

The tractor kept moving forward, and no matter how hard I pressed the brakes, it would not stop. It was then that I realised that there was more than met the eye to this driving malarkey.

It was traveling at walking pace, so it felt to me like slow motion, as it slowly edged its way towards the trees. By now I was terrified, and knew that at any moment I would be in the trees.

I still don't know why I didn't jump from the tractor as it wasn't going too fast, but for some strange reason I thought that I could still rescue myself from what was about to happen.

Well talk about being optimistic or deluded, probably both, so just a few feet away now from the banana trees and just behind them were my friends, the bees! You can imagine what was going through my mind, as flashbacks of my last encounter with these bees had come to mind.

Absolute terror would about sum it up. I was frozen with fear as by then, the front of the tractor had made contact with the first tree.

The tractor slowly impacted the tree, and to my amazement the tree started to bend as the front of the tractor slowly made its way up the trunk of the tree and the trees next to it.

Up went the tractor until the trees were bent at an almost 90 degree angle. I was expecting them to snap, but to my surprise they did not.

Instead the tractor came to rest on top of three of the trees, as the rear wheels had started to loose traction and just started to turn in the air.

It was then that one of the farm labourers came to my rescue. He had heard my screaming, and came to see what all the hullabaloo was all about.

By the look on his face I could tell that he was to put it mildly, quite shocked at the scene before him.

I don't think that he had ever seen anything like it before. There before him, was this huge tractor that was perched on top of a bunch of bent over banana trees that was still trying to move forward but was unable to get enough traction to do so.

Then on top of it was this terrified kid.

I have been forever grateful for that mans quick response. He immediately sprang into action and got me off of the tractor.

He then placed it into reverse and thank goodness, he managed to get it down from the trees.

To my amazement the trees were not too damaged, and eventually straightened themselves out.

I think it is safe to say that a major disaster was averted with no thanks to me, but with much gratitude for our farm worker.

He drove the tractor back to where it had been, before I got my hands on it, and parked it there.

I will always be grateful to him , not only for rescuing me, but also for not letting my father know!

That time I did not need the comics!

Chapter15
THE SHOOTING INCIDENTS.

It was the summer of 76 which proved to be very eventful for me. Why? Well I was able to get my hands on guns!

There were guns of all sorts and sizes. I had a ball, and quite a few frights along the way.

Growing up in KwaZulu Natal was an amazing time of my life and I will always remember it, even though I was only 8 years old when we moved there. We left when I was 10.

That time held some of the most enjoyable adventurous memories for me.

The Air Rifle: Iguanas
As a young lad of 8 years old I had imagined myself to be a great hunter as I walked around the farmlands.

One day while I was sitting in my tree house (which was my sacred domain) I had spotted a strange looking thing. It was making it's way up the trunk of a tree across from my treehouse.

On closer inspection, I was able to identify the culprit. It was a rather large Iguana that was making its way towards a birds nest to steal its eggs.

I remember thinking that I did not like the fact that this giant lizard was going to steal this mother bird's eggs, and so I loaded my air rifle and aimed at it as it made its way towards the nest.

I thought that I had better steady myself. I then pulled the trigger. Pop! it hit the thieving iguana. Immediately it lost its grip on the tree and fell to the ground.

"Yes!", I shouted, as it lay there on the ground motionless.

I had killed it, was my first thought and then to my surprise as I was watching it and wondering what to do with it. It popped onto it's feet and scurried off into the bushes and out of sight.

That was the first of many encounters with the iguanas that tried to steal the eggs from the trees.

The truth was that the air rifle did not do any real harm to them. It just gave them enough of a fright to get them to fall to the ground and then play dead.

Dollies in my Tree House!

Not long after the encounters with the
Iguanas something happened that
shocked me to my core.

One saturday afternoon I went out to the
garden and made my way to the
treehouse. As I got closer to it, to my
horror I noticed that my sister was
playing dollies in my treehouse!
This meant war! As you might have
noticed, my sister and I were not the best
of friends and

there were boundaries that I thought should never have been crossed. The treehouse was one.

The treehouse was not a place for dollies. It was my fort. My castle, my sacred place of escape.

So being the easygoing chap that I was, when I found my sister in the treehouse, I promptly invited her to leave and told her to take her dolls with her. For some unknown reason she refused. Well that was not very nice, so I asked her again, to which she was having none of it.

So the only solution was to go in and get my air rifle, and scare her into leaving the treehouse.

I stood down below and took aim. I told her "This is your last warning! Take your dollies and get out of the treehouse!" To which my wonderful sister just laughed. Her laughter was cut short when I pulled the trigger and a split second later the air was filled with a very loud screaming sound, and I knew that I was in really big trouble.

The pellet had hit it's target and now there were tears. Hers and mine. Mine, because I knew that I was going to get it big time.

Well, she got out of the treehouse with great speed, and the next thing I knew, my mother was there, the air rifle was whipped right out of my hands and I got smacked across the head. That was the last time I ever laid eyes on my air rifle again.

However, that was not the last of my adventures with Guns.

The Real Guns.

My first encounters with real guns came shortly after this incident with my sister.

The farm that bordered our farm had two children on it (a boy and a girl) whom I befriended. They were a few years older than myself. They had 50cc motor scooters, that they made their way around their farmlands on.

To me they were the cool older kids, and I loved going to their farm and hanging out with them.

One of the main reasons, was that they both had their own point 22 rifles and more importantly, they had the keys to the gun cabinet.

We would often go out into the bush and go shooting. For the most part, we did very little harm, which in itself was nothing short of a miracle. Let me tell you why.

We would go out with point 22 rifles which at close range could kill you and at best maim you. However, they were just the baby ones. I know that this may seem implausible, but this is what happened.

The oldest Kid, who was the boy who would go and get the guns from the cabinet, and we would go out with a nine millimetre pistol. A shot gun, and a magnum pistol, and the two rifles.

It was awesome!!!

One day we went out into the bush and saw some trees on a hilltop. They were full of birds and to us this was perfect for hunting. So we got our guns and started shooting at the trees. Leaves and branches fell to the ground.

I have no clue whether we hit any of the wildlife.

My guess is, that we missed, as there was no evidence laying on the ground to suggest we had succeeded.

However.... It turns out we came very close to injuring a herdsman.
We were using the shotgun which had nearly broken my shoulder when I had flown backwards after pulling the trigger.
We let off a number of rounds and then we went to the trees to inspect our handy work.

We were feeling very happy with our efforts as the trees had been shot to bits. We then saw a person on the other side of the trees coming towards us, and at first we were not to bothered, but as he got closer, we realised that we were in big trouble.

The reason was, well although we had missed all the wildlife, we had almost hit and injured this unfortunate man, who was over the rise that the trees were situated on.

When we had gotten closer we could see a very upset man who was screaming all kinds of abuse as he had came close to being seriously injured. We were horrified and he was not to happy with us, and I dare say that if we had not had guns on us, that we may have faced his wrath big time.

This did not stop him from letting us know in no uncertain terms what he thought of us. We made a hasty retreat and never heard from, or saw him again.

This did however put a dampener on our outings from then on.

Chapter16
PRICKLY PEAR TWICE.

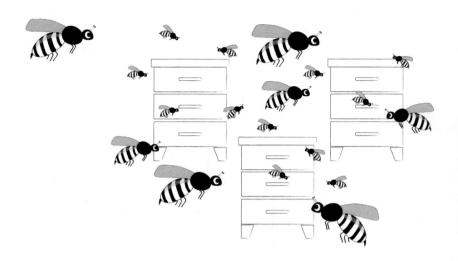

Growing up in KwaZulu Natal was one of my favourite times of my life. It was not boring living on a farm. In fact it was quite the opposite.

We had beehives on the farm and I remember the time, that my dad decided that it was time to collect the honey from the hives. He had invested in a suit that would protect him from the bees and for some strange reason, he seemed to think that I would enjoy doing it with him.

To tell the truth I was quite excited about the prospect of helping him and getting my share of the honey.

The only problem was that he had only invested in one suit and for some strange reason he thought that I would not need one. Oh no I would be fine. He had a plan.

It involved a straw hat, a netting curtain, parcel tape,an overall, rubber gloves and wellies.

When we emerged from the farmhouse, I must have looked like something out of a low budget sci fi movie.

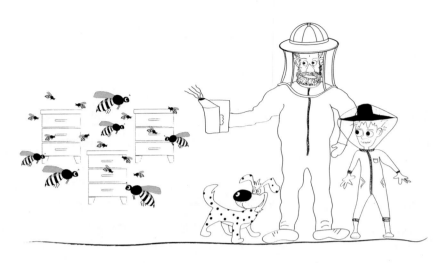

Our dog Wullie who was a dalmatian took one look at me and I'm sure I could see him smirk at me through my net curtain. Even the dog thought I looked ridiculous.

So we get to the hives, which were surrounded by those banana trees. It was sunset and my dad had the smoker, which was used to stun the bees, so that you could open the hive, and take out the honey combs and get the honey without being attacked and stung.
That was the theory anyway.

I am here to say that it did not always work out that way.

Shortly after my dad had started to smoke them, I heard a bee buzzing around my head, and thought that I would be safe.

It was then, that I discovered that my mom had not taped the curtain well enough to stop the bees from getting inside my facial area.

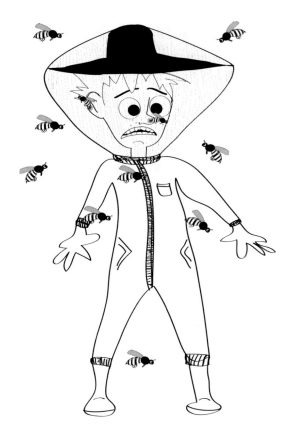

So the first one got in and then another, and another not long after that. I felt the first stab of sharp pain as I got stung on my neck. I promptly started to smack my face to kill the bee.

Then another, and another stung me..

By then I must have been frantic as Wullie our dog thought that this was a fun game and started to bark and jump up on me to play.

My head gear had filled up with bees, and by then I started to run toward the house. It had grown dark and was almost pitch black outside. I dropped my torch and I ran screaming with my arms flailing madly as I ran through the woods.

I could not see where I was going, and
ran smack bang into tree after tree. I
could feel bees being squashed as I hit
them.

By now I could feel the bees stinging my ears, nose mouth neck and shoulders and even my back. All the while Wullie was barking and enjoying the crazy new game.

After what seemed an eternity I made it to our front door and was screaming my head off. My mom took one look at me and realised what was going on. I was covered in bees. She grabbed the fly swatter and swatted them and then got my clothes off. There I sat with all the bee stings on my body. My mom took a pair of tweezers and plucked them all out of my upper body.

As it turned out, it was the night that we discovered that I was not allergic to bee stings, even though I looked like a prickly pear from the waist up!

I still love honey, but I have never harvested honey since that painful night.

I would like to tell you that was the last time that I was seriously stung. But alas there were other times.

As a young boy growing up in the subtropical natal climate of South Africa I was accustomed to wearing only shorts and a t shirt.

No shoes were worn as we never wore them except when we went to school. As soon as we got home, the shoes were flung off and outside we would go bare foot. The result was that the souls of our feet were as hard as old leather.

It was a beautiful summers day on the farm, so I decided to head on over to our neighbours farm for some shooting.

I had made my way through the fields of waist high grass and all was well with the world until I started to feel this strange sensation on my bare legs and feet.

At first I did not register that I was actually being stung by a swarm of wasps.

They stung me so fast and frequently that at first I thought that I had a case of severe pins and needles in my legs.

It turned out that the wasp nest was on the ground and was hidden in the tall grass and yes, you guessed it, I had stood right on top of it and didn't even notice it, until the pins and needles started to feel quite painful.

When I looked at my legs I was shocked to see them covered in wasps. I was off like a shot, my arms flailing. I smacked my legs, and screamed at the top of my lungs all the while as I tried to get rid of the wasps.

I ran all the way home and jumped into the duck pond to get rid of them. I made it into the house and I looked like a prickly pear from the waist down.

Chapter17
THE WEEKEND PARTIES ON THE FARM.

Shortly after the lost teef incident, we moved from Sutton Park to a farm in Cato Ridge and it was then that the weekend parties really started to get wild.

Now that we lived in a remote area it seemed like a grand idea, to not only have parties on the weekends, but it was also time to spice things up! How?

Well my dad and his friends thought it would be a great place to have shooting parties. These were parties with guns. Yes anyone who had a gun would be welcome to come and consume massive amounts of food, and even more alcohol, and then out would come the guns, and all hell would break loose.

I am still amazed to this day that no one was injured or killed during those times.

Me especially, as I was the one who would be responsible for placing the bottles and cans on top of a stone wall for them to shoot at.

My favourite part was sitting behind the wall while they in their drunken states, were trying to shoot the bottles and cans of the wall.

I loved the sound of the bullets whizzing over my head, as they were amazingly able to hit these targets despite the fact that they could hardly walk in a straight line!

For me this was a massive rush, and I couldn't get the bottles up quick enough for them to have another go.

It was on one of these occasions that my very drunk father decided that he wanted to show off to to all of his friends that he was a great cowboy and that he was an amazing horse rider.

The only problem was that the horse he wanted to ride was mine and was now rather old and not really up to taking his weight which was quite considerable.

So my father called me in front of all his drunken friends and told me to go and saddle up Tailstar (my horse).

I was not very keen but I knew better than to argue with him, when he was in that state.

Remember I said earlier that my dad looked like Hagar the Horrible! Well it was like seeing Hagar the Horrible with his big belly trying to ride my poor old horse.

So I decided to teach him a lesson that he would never forget. I thought to myself "I will saddle the horse for him but I wouldn't tighten up the saddle strap".

The plan was that if he went off too fast the saddle would twist around and my father would end up under the horses belly.

205

Well I have to say It worked out even better than I had anticipated.

Picture the scene: my father who was in a very drunken state climbed onto the horse and in his usual arrogant fashion set of down our two mile long driveway.

So off he went at quite a considerable pace. I started counting 10, 9, 8, 7, 6, 5, 4, any second now! And then as I anticipated there was a loud shriek and some choice words of displeasure followed and then silence.

I knew then that I was in big trouble, but it was worth it!

Shortly after the horse appeared at the top of the driveway and then after about five minutes my father also appeared looking like a bright red tomato and with rage in his eyes.

There he stood in his denim shorts and T-shirt which hardly covered his beer belly. His elbows and knees were skint and he was staggering and quite battered and bruised.

The look in his eyes told me all I needed to know. I was off like a shot.

I am convinced that the reason I am still alive today and writing this was because his guests thought it was hilarious and they protected me as they calmed him down.

Because of them I lived to fight another day.

It was shortly after these events that my Father decided that it was no longer safe for us to stay in South Africa. There had been political upheaval which he thought endangered us so he sent my mother, sister and I back to Scotland.

This led to some rather crazy adventures that resulted in me being chased by the police and...... Well that's another story for another book.

Look out for JUNGLE SWINGER the Scottish Years!

Scotland here we come!